"Thou Shalt Never Quit"

The Story of General Daniel "Chappie" James Jr.

"Thou Shalt Never Quit"
The Story of General Daniel "Chappie" James Jr.

Written & Illustrated by Dr. Sharon Gaston
Cover design by
damian@dazz.media

Published by Doc Publishing

First Printing: 2020

ISBN: 978-0-9967370-8-1

Doc Publishing
P.O. Box 7503
New Castle, PA 16107

docpublishing@yahoo.com

Ordering Information:

Special discounts are available on quantity purchases by educators, corporations, associations, and others. For details, contact the publisher at the above listed address.

U.S. trade bookstores and wholesalers: Please contact Doc Publishing at the above address or email.

This book is dedicated to my nephews, Donte Jr. & Nickolas Morrissette (two aspiring pilots) & My Dear Friends, Cliff & Lydia Curtis

Table of Contents

Introduction

Before March 14, 1941, there was no such thing as African American aviators in the United States Armed Forces. Everything changed with the arrival of the Tuskegee Airmen.

The Tuskegee Airmen were a group of African American men who

flew for the United States
during World War II. They trained
at the Tuskegee Army Airfield
located in Tuskegee, Alabama.
These courageous trailblazers flew
more than 15,000 individual missions
in Europe and North Africa.
Because of their outstanding service,
they earned more than 150
Distinguished Flying Crosses.

The success of the Tuskegee
Airmen was an important step
forward in preparing the United
States of America for the racial
integration of the military.

This book is meant to honor the
life and accomplishments of one of
those pioneering Tuskegee Airmen
who became the first African
American four-star general in the
armed forces.

This is the story of General
Daniel "Chappie" James Jr.

Chapter 1

Daniel James Jr. was the 17th and last child born to Daniel James Sr. and Lillie Anna James on February 11, 1920 in segregated Pensacola, Florida. They lovingly called him, Baby Dan.

His parents had previously lost 10 children before he was born due to a lack of access to basic health care. On the day he was born, his father exclaimed with bliss, "Look Lillie Anna. Look how Baby Dan's eyes sparkle!" Mrs. James looked at her last child.

She smiled and said, "Yes, Dan. They sparkle with the glow of a prosperous future."

Baby Dan inherited the nickname, *Chappie*, from his older brother, Charles, who was also called Chappie as a term of endearment.

The elder Chappie was a football star at Florida Agricultural & Mechanical University (FAMU).

Chappie's parents raised him in a loving home, built with his father's own hands. Mr. James diligently emphasized thorough academic excellence and having great character to his children.

Though Chappie grew up in the Jim Crow south, his parents constantly expressed to all of their children that they were not inferior to anyone and encouraged them to face the obstacles of racism and discrimination head on.

Mr. and Mrs. James instilled in their children a sense of freedom and fair play, the gift of laughter and to stay positive and prepared in any situation.

All of these characteristics would later be instrumental to Chappie during his illustrious military career.

Chapter 2

Disappointed with the education that her children received in the public-school system, Chappie's mother, Lillie Anna, who was a teacher, founded her own private school. She taught her children and other black children in Pensacola. She ran her school for 52 years. Mrs. James' eleventh commandment and school mantra were, *Thou Shalt Never Quit.*

Thou Shalt Never Quit

Mrs. James would always say to her children and her students, "Don't stand there banging on the door of opportunity, then when someone opens it, you say, wait a minute, I got to get my bags." She went on to say, "You be prepared with your bags of knowledge, your patriotism, your honor, and when somebody opens the door, you charge in."

Chapter 3

Mr. James Sr., who worked for the local gas company, constantly stressed to his children the importance of being high achievers. He would tell them, "Give your all, and then some, to the task at hand."

Chappie used to reflect on how his father held very high expectations for all of his children and would not accept anything less.

"Son, did you finish that task I gave you?" "Yes sir. I finished it," Chappie answered. His father asked, "Did you give 110%?" "Yes sir, Pop. I sure did," Chappie said proudly. "Good. Now let's start over."

Chapter 4

Chappie wanted to be a pilot ever since the sight of roaring airplanes from the Pensacola Navy Base captured his attention. He would tell his friends, "Wow! Look at that plane go! I want to be a pilot when I grow up."

His friends would laugh and say, "Man, that's impossible. You are black. You can't be a pilot, Chappie!" Chappie would look at his doubting friends and remember his parents' teachings and say, "Watch!"

Chapter 5

In 1933, Chappie attended Washington High School and sang in the chorus and glee club. He was a member of the football team, too.

His coach noted that he was enthusiastic and steadily improved his football skills through hard work and perseverance. Chappie's fellow teammates were inspired by his positive spirit, as well.

During this time, Chappie's new principal, Mr. Vernon McDaniel, made a lasting impression upon him. Mr. McDaniel was a dedicated educator who held tall expectations for his students and boldly met with the superintendent of schools to request needed funding for Washington High School.

Mr. McDaniel developed academic curricula to ensure his students received rigorous teachings in all disciplines similar to the white students.

Mr. McDaniel was an average-size man who carried around a strap at school. He was even known to drive around in the black sections of town on school nights checking to see if his students were in the dance halls or popular hang-out spots. The students were known to say, "Run! Here comes Mr. Mac!"

Chapter 6

Tragedy struck the James family in the spring of 1937 when James Sr. died before Chappie graduated high school.

Although the James family was devastated, courage, faith and determination carried them through the loss of their beloved father.

Chappie was worried that he would not be able to go away to college after his father's death. However, his siblings and his mother rallied around him to make sure he would have enough money to attend school.

"Don't worry, baby brother. We will all make sure that you have the money for college."

Chapter 7

By 1937, the strapping 6-foot 4-inch Chappie earned a football scholarship to attend Tuskegee Institute located in Tuskegee, Alabama. It was founded by educator Booker T. Washington in 1881.

In addition, he was given the opportunity to enroll in a government-sponsored flight program named the Civilian Pilot Training Program (CPTP).

It was during this time that Chappie also became a stunt flyer.

Unfortunately, two months before Chappie was supposed to graduate from Tuskegee, he was suspended for fighting. He soon learned how one mistake or lapse in judgment could cost him all that he had worked for. It was now relevant to him that not displaying good character could ruin his hopes and dreams. This hard lesson motivated Chappie to get on the *straight and narrow.*

He recognized that reckless behavior, such as fighting, would hinder his aspirations and disappoint his family, as well as himself. Chappie buckled down and decided to live life with integrity and the noble virtues that were instilled in him as a child.

It would be twenty-five years later before Chappie would earn his bachelor of science degree in physical education.

Chappie also received his commission as a 2nd Lieutenant in the U.S. Army Air Corps and earned pilot wings at the Tuskegee Army Airfield in Tuskegee, Alabama on July 28, 1943.

He became a flight instructor at Tuskegee Institute where he became, and also trained, the famed *Tuskegee Airmen* during World War II.

Chapter 8

In 1938, Chappie met Dorothy Watkins in Tuskegee at a Memorial Day dance. The two fell in love and wed November 3, 1943.

Chappie and Dorothy had a daughter and two sons. Their daughter, who was the oldest of the three siblings, was named Danice. She later became a nurse at Sacred Heart Hospital located in Pensacola, Florida.

Chappie's eldest son was named Daniel James III, who, like his father, became a general in the Air Force. Claude, the youngest son, was named after one of Chappie's dearest friends, Claude "Spud" Taylor.

Chapter 9

As a member of the Army Air Corps Aviation Cadet Program, Chappie did not see air combat until the Korean War.

Chapter 10

President Harry S. Truman integrated the United States military in 1949. Chappie James still experienced copious amounts of racism that threatened to obscure his military career. But his determination and persistence to give

100% carried him over the brazen, racial barriers that he faced daily.

When Chappie was stationed in the Philippines as flight leader for the 12th Fighter Bomber Squadron, the white servicemen would not speak to him. He eventually met a kind and gregarious fellow officer from Texas named, Claude "Spud" Taylor, who had the same interest in music as he had.

"What? You can sing and play the drums, Chappie? I play the saxophone!" Claude said excitedly. The two musician friends found a piano player and formed a musical trio that many people enjoyed.

Spud Taylor even intervened on little Danice's behalf when neighborhood kids had bullied her because she was black. Spud went to each of the children's homes and spoke with their parents and the harassment ceased immediately.

Sadly, Claude Taylor was killed during combat in Korea and Chappie honored the memory of his friend by naming his second son after him.

Chapter 11

Chappie James left for Korea in 1950 and flew 101 combat missions. He experienced his first genuine dogfight while flying ground support.

Chappie was jumped by jet-powered MiG's and later said, "I maneuvered around until U.S. jets arrived for backup and believe I hit and damaged one MiG as it was leaving." His training, courage, preparedness and execution of tasks are what sustained him during the melee.

Upon returning from Korea, Chappie James' military experience flourished.

In 1953, he became a squadron commander, a staff officer at the Pentagon and European Service at Royal Air Force Bentwaters, England.

During the 1960s, he attained a promotion as deputy commander for operations at Davis-Monthan Air Force Base in Arizona.

Following this, Chappie James was sent to Vietnam where he flew over 70 combat missions in countries that reached from India to China.

While in Vietnam, he was victorious in one of the greatest fighter battles of the Vietnam War.

Later, he was stationed as Vice Wing Commander at Eglin Air Force Base in Fort Walton Beach, Florida.

Chapter 12

From fall 1969 until spring 1970, Chappie directed an operation to shut down Wheeler Air Base in Libya where he had a clash with Libyan Dictator, Muammar Gaddafi.

His success in this face-off prompted President Richard Nixon to nominate him for Brigadier General. Chappie was offered the position of Deputy Assistant Secretary of Defense, Public Affairs, but was not sure he wanted the job.

"Mr. President, I am a fighter pilot. Not a specialist of public affairs." Nixon responded to him. "Your days as a fighter pilot are behind you now and you will be perfect in public affairs."

Chappie relented and accepted the position. He was later designated Principal Deputy Assistant Secretary of Defense, Public Affairs in 1973.

Chapter 13

Chappie was a commanding and eloquent speaker who spoke out vigorously in defense of the Vietnam War. His powerfully patriotic and motivational speeches connected with disgruntled African American servicemen, military wives as well as high school and college students.

A military widow said after one of his speeches, "General James, you are such an exciting orator. Thank you for your service."

"Thank you for your kind words," Chappie responded.

In 1974, another promotion elevated Chappie to Lieutenant General, and in 1975 he became the first African American four-star General in the U.S. military.

Chappie then went on to command the North American Aerospace Defense Command (NORAD).

This was an historical achievement. At this time in history, General "Chappie" James was one of the most powerful men----of any color.

Chapter 14

After being recognized with his his fourth star, Chappie James shared some words of wisdom with the audience. "This promotion is important to me by the effect it will have on some kid on a hot sidewalk in some ghetto. If my making an advancement can serve as some kind of spark to some young black or other minority, it will be worth all the years and all the blood and sweat it took getting here."

Chappie's hometown of Pensacola, Florida celebrated *General "Chappie" James Day* with a parade in his honor.

Chapter 15

Chappie James lived through a tumultuous and volatile era filled with racism and bigotry. He rejected it when some African Americans voiced criticism of his preeminent status in the military.

Chappie James responded to his critics when he said, "People don't sometimes look at the sum of my life. I am a Negro and, therefore, I am subject to their constant harangue. I suffered through years of dealing with discriminatory practices in the military. I did not limit myself to being just a black leader, a leader of whites or a Catholic leader. Leaders are made and not born. They make themselves through total dedication and preparation. I've fought in three wars and three more wouldn't be too many to defend my country. I love America and as she has weaknesses or ills, I'll hold her hand."

Chapter 16

General Daniel "Chappie" James Jr. retired from military service in 1978. Less than a month after his retirement, he suddenly passed away from a heart attack. Chappie James was buried at Arlington National Cemetery with full military honors. He has left behind a legacy of leadership, patriotism, courage, dedication and high moral character.

In May 1987, Tuskegee Institute
dedicated their Center for
Aerospace Science and Health
Education in his honor.

In 1996, Pensacola native, Cliff Curtis, along with Mike Griffin, Craig Abernathy and Mike Fowlkes, were four naval flight instructors who had been recently hired by the commercial airline industry.

The four pilots conceptualized and opened the General Daniel "Chappie" James Jr. Flight Academy in Pensacola, Florida to introduce school-aged children to the aviation community and career possibilities in the field.

A museum was erected in June 2018 in Chappie James' hometown of Pensacola so future generations will have the opportunity to learn about his eminent legacy.

The flight academy, named in his honor, is now housed at the museum which is located on the same land as his childhood home.

In addition, the city of Pensacola is in the process of renaming the Three-Mile Bridge the *General Daniel "Chappie" James Jr. Memorial Bridge*. The Three-Mile Bridge runs between downtown Pensacola and Gulf Breeze, Florida.

This dedication is set to take place in the year 2021.

Chapter 17

General Daniel "Chappie" James Jr. lived a life full of dignity and amazing accomplishments. His fortitude, patriotism and natural leadership abilities married with the steadfast philosophy of his parents, won him the respect of many, including presidents, military dignitaries, and school children.

Chappie was affectionately called the "Black Eagle" by his fellow pilots because of his special skills in the aerial combat arena, as well as his flawless ethics of achievement, hard work, and self-assurance.

His mother's 11th commandment, *"Thou Shalt Never Quit,"* was evident throughout his life.

General Daniel "Chappie" James Jr. truly did personify the American dream.

Critical Thinking Questions

1. What challenges did Chappie James face during his life and how did he work to overcome them?

2. Who were the people that made an impact on Chappie James and how did their impact influence his life?

3. Name ways in which Chappie James displayed bravery in this story.

4. If you could ask Chappie James a question, what would it be?

5. Name some of Chappie James' many accomplishments?

6. Why do you think the author entitled the book *Thou Shalt Never Quit*?

7. In what ways does the story of
   General Daniel "Chappie" James
   Jr. remind you of other books
   you have read? Discuss.

8. Do you think that General
   Daniel "Chappie" James Jr.
   should be considered a
   hometown hero in Pensacola,
   Florida? Explain.

GLOSSARY

1. **Arlington National Cemetery** - United States military cemetery in Arlington County, Virginia, where dead servicemen and women are buried.

2. **Civilian Pilot Training Program (CPTP)** – Flight training program (1938–1944) sponsored by the U. S. government with the stated purpose of increasing the number of civilian pilots, though having a clear impact on military preparedness.

3. **Commander** - A person in authority, especially over a body of troops or a military operation.

4. **Curricula** - The subjects comprising a course of study in a school or college.

5.   **Dignity** - The state or quality of being worthy of honor or respect.

6.   **Disgruntled** - Angry or dissatisfied.

7.   **Discrimination** - The unjust or prejudicial treatment of different categories of people or things, especially on the grounds of race, age, or sex.

8.   **General** - A commander of an army, or an army officer of very high rank.

9.   **Gregarious** - A person fond of company; sociable, friendly, outgoing.

10.   **Jim Crow** - Laws that were state and local which enforced racial segregation in the Southern United States. All were enacted in the late 19th

and early 20th centuries by white Democratic-dominated state legislatures after the Reconstruction period. The laws were enforced until 1965.

11.	**Lieutenant General** - A commissioned officer in the US Army, Air Force, or Marine Corps ranking above major general and below general.

12.	**MiG** - Mikoyan-i-Gurevich Design Bureau is a military aircraft design bureau, primarily designing fighter aircraft.

13.	**Patriotism** - The quality of being patriotic; devotion to and vigorous support for one's country.

14.   **Perseverance** - Persistence in doing something despite difficulty or delay in achieving success.

15.   **Prosperous** - Successful in material terms; flourishing financially.

16.   **Racism** - Prejudice, discrimination, or antagonism directed against someone of a different race based on the belief that one's own race is superior.

17.   **Squadron** - In the air force, army aviation, or naval aviation, it is a unit comprising a number of military aircraft and their aircrews.

18.   **Straight and Narrow** - The honest and morally acceptable way of living.

19.   **Thou Shalt Never Quit** –
This was Lilli Anna's, Chappie
James' mother's, 11th
commandment that she stated
frequently as words of
inspiration to her children and
her students.

20.   **Tuskegee Airmen** - The
first black military aviators in
the U.S. Army Air Corps (AAC),
a precursor of the U.S. Air
Force. Trained at
the Tuskegee Army Airfield in
Alabama, they flew more than
15,000 individual operations in
Europe and North Africa
during World War II.

21.   **Tuskegee Institute** – Now known as Tuskegee University, is a private, historically black university (HBCU) located in Tuskegee, Alabama. It was established by Lewis Adams and Booker T. Washington. The university was home to World War II's Tuskegee Airmen.

About the Author

At the age of 10, Dr. Sharon Gaston moved to Pensacola, Florida where her father was stationed at the Naval Air Station and her mother was a civilian employee.

Sharon attended Escambia County Public Schools and graduated from Booker T. Washington High School In 1983.

Dr. Gaston received an associate's degree from Pensacola Junior College in 1987 and earned a bachelor's degree in Elementary Education from the University of West Florida in 1990. Two years later she relocated with her daughter, Courtney, to the state of Maryland.

In 1997, she received a master's degree in Reading Education and a doctorate degree in Educational Leadership and Supervision in 2007 from Bowie State University in Bowie, Maryland.

Dr. Gaston has served as assistant principal, Title I home visiting teacher, classroom teacher and is currently a reading specialist in Arlington, Virginia.

She has written over 30 children's books and plays and performs as a professional storyteller. Dr. Gaston lives with her husband, Richard Halttunen, in Potomac, Maryland where they collaborate on many writing projects.

BIBLIOGRAPHY

Bracey, Ernest N. (2015). *Daniel "Chappie" James: The First African American Four-Star General.* McFarland.

Greenspan, Jessy (2016, March 18). *The Birth of the Tuskegee Airmen.* History Stories. Retrieved from https://www.history.com/news/the-birth-of-the-tuskegee-airmen

History.comeditors (2020, January) *Tuskegee Airmen.* Retrieved from https://www.history.com/topics/world-war-ii/tuskegee-airmen

Lexico U. S. Dictionary (2020). Powered by Oxford. Retrieved from English Dictionary, Thesaurus, & Grammar Help | Lexico.com.

McGovern, James R. (2002). *Black Eagle: General Daniel "Chappie" James, Jr.:* University of Alabama Press.

Moye, Todd (2010) *Freedom Flyers: The Tuskegee Airmen of World War II*, New York: Oxford University Press.

Phelps, Aelfred J. (1992) *Chappie: America's First Black Four-star General : The Life and Times of Daniel James, Jr.* Presidio.

Redtailadmin (2015, October 1). *America's Tribute to the Tuskegee Airmen; Daniel Chappie James Jr.* Retrieved from https://www.redtail.org/portraits-of-tuskegee-airmen-daniel-chappie-james-jr/

United States Air Force (1978, January). *General Daniel James Jr.* Retrieved from https://www.af.mil/About-Us/Biographies/Display/Article/106647/general-daniel-james-jr/

Wikipedia (February, 2020). Daniel James Jr. Retrieved from https://en.wikipedia.org/wiki/Daniel_James_Jr.

www.ingramcontent.com/pod-product-compliance
Lightning Source LLC
LaVergne TN
LVHW091209080426
835509LV00006B/908